THE MUSIC OF MOTIVATION

A BRIEF GUIDE TO INSPIRATIONAL FILM SONGS

DR. JAGADEESH PILLAI

|| Dedicated to All Motivation Seekers Around The World ||

Contents

Contents

PRAYER

**"Om Poornamadah Poornamidam Poornat
Poornamudachyate,Poornasya Poornamaadaya
Poornamevavavashishyate,Om Shantih, Shantih, Shantih"**

*The literal interpretation of this mantra is: That which is
Absolute, This which is Absolute, Absolute arises from Absolute,
If Absolute is removed from Absolute, Absolute remains
OM Peace, Peace, Peace.*

About The Author

Dr. Jagadeesh Pillai is a renowned Guinness World Record holder, writer, and researcher hailing from Varanasi, also known as the abode of Lord Shiva. With a Ph.D. in Vedic Science and a range of creative ideas and achievements, he is a true polymath. He is the author of more than 100 books including Research Publications. Although his roots can be traced back to Kerala, the people of Varanasi hold him in high regard and affectionately consider him one of their own.

Dr. Pillai has achieved four Guinness World Records in the following subjects:

1. "Script to Screen" - In this record, Dr. Pillai produced and directed an animation film within the shortest time possible, breaking the previous record set by Canadians. He has also received numerous national and international awards and recognitions for this achievement.

2. Longest Line of Postcards - For this record, Dr. Pillai created a line of 16,300 postcards on the occasion of the 163rd anniversary of Indian Postal Day. The event also included a questionnaire about the Indian flag.

3. Largest Poster Awareness Campaign - Dr. Pillai designed an awareness campaign on the subject of "Beti Bachao - Beti Padhao" (Save the Girl Child - Educate the Girl Child)

to achieve this record.

4. Largest Envelope - In tribute to the Indian Prime Minister's "Make in India" initiative, Dr. Pillai created a 4000 square meter envelope using waste paper to achieve this record.

5. Attempted - 70000 Candles on a 210 kg Cake - To celebrate the 70th Indian Independence Day, Dr. Pillai attempted to light 70,000 candles on a 210 kg cake, which was recorded in World Records India.

6. Attempted - Documentary on Dhamek Stupa of Sarnath in 17 Languages - Dr. Pillai attempted to create a documentary on the Dhamek Stupa of Sarnath, dubbing it in 17 different languages. The result of this attempt is currently awaiting confirmation from the Guinness World Records.

Dr. Pillai is skilled in teaching the Bhagavad Gita, a Hindu scripture, and is popular among young people. He has helped many young people improve their lives through his motivational teachings.

In addition to teaching, he has composed and sung

numerous Sanskrit Bhajans and patriotic songs.

He has also written and directed several short films and documentaries for awareness campaigns, and has volunteered with the police in both UP and Kerala to spread awareness about various issues through videos and photography.

He has a goal of writing thousands of books on Indian culture, Indian temples, and the lives of extraordinary people. Incredibly, he has produced and directed over 100 documentaries about the city of Varanasi, all on his own.

He has also helped and guided more than 25 boys and girls to achieve world records through creative and innovative methods. He is a multifaceted person who uses his intellect and the blessings given to him by God to excel in various areas. He is both a teacher and a student, always learning and teaching, and is able to master any subject he comes across.

He is a selfless social activist and motivational speaker who has overcome struggles and failures to become a successful and enthusiastic individual with a rich life experience.

In addition to his work with the Bhagavad Gita, he is also an efficient Tarot card reader, Astro-Vastu consultant, and a talented singer and composer. He has sung the entire Ram Charita Manas and Bhagavad Gita in his own compositions, and has sung the phrase "Lokah Samastha Sukhino Bhavantu" in 50 different languages. He is currently working on a detailed and scientific study of Vedas, Upanishads, Puranas, and the Bhagavad Gita. He has also composed and sung the Hanuman Chalisa and Gayatri Mantra in 108 and 1008 different compositions, respectively.

Awards - Four Times Guinness World Records, Winner of Mahatma Gandhi Vishwa Shanti Puraskar , Mahatma Gandhi Global Peace Ambassador, Kashi Ratna Award, Dr. APJ Abdul Kalam Motivational Person of the Year 2017, Mother Teresa Award, Indira Gandhi Priyadarshini Award, Bharat Vikas Ratna Award, Udyog Ratna Award, Vigyan Prasar Award, Poorvanchal Ratn Samman.

PREFACE

Motivational songs in Bollywood films have long been a source of inspiration and motivation for audiences. From the uplifting beats to the powerful lyrics, these songs have the power to encourage and motivate even the most discouraged of individuals. This book provides an in-depth look into the world of motivational songs from films, offering a comprehensive guide to more than thirty five of the most inspiring and energizing compositions. Each song is accompanied by a brief overview, providing readers with a quick reference guide to the best of Bollywood's motivational music. Whether you're looking for a pick-me-up or a source of inspiration, this book is sure to provide the perfect soundtrack to your journey.

The book "Brief of Motivational Film Songs - ***"The Music of Motivation: A Brief Guide to Inspirational Film Songs"*** is an attempt to compile a comprehensive collection of the most powerful and inspiring songs from Bollywood films. The films covered in this book are not only entertaining but also provide a window into the richness of energetic compositions and perfect lyrics combination to encourage and motivate any disappointed person.

The book is organized in a way that makes it easy for readers to find the songs they are looking for. Each chapter is dedicated to a specific film, and within each chapter, a brief summary of the film's plot and the significance of its songs is provided.

In this book, I have covered more than thirty five films, each of them having at least one song that can motivate people to work hard and make their dreams come true. The films and songs covered in this book are a reflection of the versatility and diversity of Bollywood. From classic films of the past to modern hits, we have included a wide range of films to appeal to a diverse readership.

The book is not only a quick reference guide for readers who are looking for inspiration and motivation but also a source of entertainment for those who love Bollywood films and music. I hope that this book will become a valuable addition to your library and that the songs and films covered within its pages will provide you with the motivation and inspiration you need to achieve your goals.

I am confident that this book will be a source of inspiration and motivation for readers of all ages and backgrounds. We hope that it will inspire you to take action and make positive changes in your life and career.

So let's dive into the world of Bollywood films and discover the power of motivational songs!

Koi Kahe Kehta Rahe

"Koi Kahe Kehta Rahe" from Dil Chahta Hai is a song that speaks to the human desire to be true to oneself and to live life on one's own terms. The lyrics of the song urge the listener to not be swayed by the opinions of others and to follow one's own heart. The song encourages the listener to be confident in themselves and to not be afraid to take risks and pursue their dreams, even if it means going against the norm or defying societal expectations. The upbeat tempo and catchy melody of the song help to convey the message of positivity and self-empowerment.

II

Suno Gaur Se Duniya Walon

"Suno Gaur Se Duniya Walon" from Dus is a song that promotes the importance of standing up for oneself and speaking out against injustice and oppression. The lyrics of the song urge the listener to not be afraid to raise their voice against those who seek to silence or oppress them, and to fight for their rights and beliefs. The song also encourages unity and togetherness, as it encourages people to come together and support one another in the face of adversity. The fast-paced beat and energetic tone of the song help to convey the message of strength, courage, and determination.

III

Chak De from Chak De India

"Chak De" from Chak De India is a song that serves as a powerful anthem of motivation and inspiration. The lyrics of the song urge the listener to never give up on their dreams and to strive for success no matter the odds. The song also promotes the idea of teamwork and unity, as it encourages the listener to come together with their fellow players and work towards a common goal. The fast-paced beat and rousing melody of the song help to convey the message of determination and perseverance.

IV

Ae Watan from Raazi

"Ae Watan" from Raazi is a patriotic song that speaks to the sacrifices and struggles of the brave people who fought to protect their country. The lyrics of the song pay tribute to the sacrifices made by the soldiers and their families, and express gratitude towards them. The song also promotes the idea of unity and togetherness in the face of adversity, encouraging all citizens to stand together in defense of their country. The emotive melody, powerful vocals, and patriotic lyrics of the song help to convey the message of love for the country and respect for the sacrifices made for it.

V

"Galliyan" from Ek Villain

"Galliyan" from Ek Villain is a song that speaks to the importance of never giving up on love, no matter how difficult the journey may be. The song is composed by Ankit Tiwari and sung by him. The lyrics of the song urge the listener to never give up on their love and to always keep fighting for it, even in the face of adversity. The song also promotes the idea of hope and perseverance, as it encourages the listener to never lose faith in the power of love. The slow and emotive melody, coupled with the powerful vocals, help to convey the message of never giving up on love and always fighting for it.

VI

"Zinda" from Bhag Milkha Bhag

"Zinda" from Bhag Milkha Bhag is a song that showcases the motivational aspect of never giving up and always pushing yourself to be the best version of yourself, no matter the circumstances. The song is composed by Shankar-Ehsaan-Loy and sung by Shankar Mahadevan. The lyrics of the song urge the listener to never give up on their dreams and to always strive to be the best version of themselves, even in the face of adversity. The song also promotes the idea of determination and perseverance, as it encourages the listener to keep pushing forward no matter how difficult the journey may be. The fast-paced beat and powerful vocals of the song help to convey the message of never giving up and always pushing

oneself to be the best.

ॐ

VII

Jai Ho

"Jai Ho" from Slumdog Millionaire is a song that serves as a powerful anthem of hope and perseverance, composed by A. R. Rahman and sung by Sukhwinder Singh, Tanvi Shah, Mahalaxmi Iyer, Vijay Prakash. The lyrics of the song urge the listener to never give up on their dreams and to always strive for success no matter the odds. The song also promotes the idea of unity and togetherness, as it encourages the listener to come together with others to achieve a common goal. The fast-paced beat and rousing melody of the song help to convey the message of determination and perseverance, which are the key to achieve the goal.

VIII
Roar

"Roar" from Tiger Zinda Hai is a song that promotes the idea of strength, courage and determination, composed by Vishal-Shekhar and sung by Vishal Dadlani. The lyrics of the song urge the listener to be confident in themselves, and to not be afraid to take risks and pursue their dreams, even if it means going against the norm or defying societal expectations. The song also speaks to the importance of standing up for oneself and speaking out against injustice and oppression. The fast-paced beat and energetic tone of the song help to convey the message of strength, courage, and determination, and give the listener a boost of motivation to face the challenges.

IX

Chale Chalo from Lagaan

"Chale Chalo" from Lagaan is a song that serves as a powerful anthem of motivation and inspiration, composed by A.R. Rahman and sung by Srinivas, A.R. Rahman. The lyrics of the song urge the listener to never give up and to always strive for success, no matter the odds. The song also promotes the idea of teamwork and unity, as it encourages the listener to come together with their fellow players and work towards a common goal. The fast-paced beat and rousing melody of the song help to convey the message of determination and perseverance, which are key in achieving the goal.

X

Mera Rang De Basanti Chola

"Mera Rang De Basanti Chola" from The Legend of Bhagat Singh is a song that speaks to the sacrifices and struggles of the brave people who fought for freedom and rights, composed by Ajay-Atul and sung by Sukhwinder Singh. The lyrics of the song pay tribute to the sacrifices made by the freedom fighters and their families, and express gratitude towards them. The song also promotes the idea of unity and togetherness in the face of adversity, encouraging all citizens to stand together for the rights and freedom. The emotive melody and powerful vocals help to convey the message of love for the country and respect for the sacrifices made for it.

XI

Aashayein from Iqbal

"Aashayein" from Iqbal is a song that showcases the motivational aspect of never giving up, composed by Salim-Sulaiman and sung by KK. The lyrics of the song urge the listener to always keep hope and never give up, even in the face of adversity, because you never know when a change in luck will occur. The song also promotes the idea of determination and perseverance, as it encourages the listener to keep pushing forward no matter how difficult the journey may be. The slow and emotive melody, coupled with the powerful vocals, help to convey the message of hope and perseverance in the face of adversity.

XII

Ab Tumhare Hawale

"Ab Tumhare Hawale Watan Sathiyo" from Ab Tumhare Hawale Watan Sathiyo is a patriotic song that speaks to the sacrifices and struggles of the brave soldiers who fought to protect their country. The song is composed by Anu Malik and sung by Hariharan, Sonu Nigam, Roop Kumar Rathod, and Sadhana Sargam. The lyrics of the song pay tribute to the sacrifices made by the soldiers and their families, and express gratitude towards them. The song also promotes the idea of unity and togetherness in the face of adversity, encouraging all citizens to stand together in defense of their country. The emotive melody, powerful vocals, and patriotic lyrics of the song help to convey the message of love for the country and respect for the sacrifices

made for it.

XIII

Apni To Jaise Taise

"Apni To Jaise Taise" from Laawaris is a song that speaks to the importance of living life on one's own terms and not being afraid to be different, composed by Kalyanji-Anandji and sung by Kishore Kumar. The lyrics of the song urge the listener to be true to themselves and to not be swayed by the opinions of others. The song also encourages the listener to be confident in themselves and to not be afraid to take risks and pursue their dreams, even if it means going against the norm or defying societal expectations. The upbeat tempo and catchy melody of the song help to convey the message of positivity and self-empowerment.

XIV

Jee Le Zaraa from Talash

"Jee Le Zaraa" from Talaash is a song that promotes the idea of living life to the fullest and making the most of every moment, composed by Ram Sampath and sung by Sona Mohapatra. The lyrics of the song urge the listener to embrace every opportunity, to live in the present, and to not be afraid to take risks. The song also encourages the listener to enjoy life and to not be bogged down by fear or regrets. The upbeat tempo and catchy melody of the song help to convey the message of enjoying life and embracing every moment.

XV

Jeena Jeena from Badlapur

"Jeena Jeena" from Badlapur is a song that showcases the importance of moving on from the past, composed by Sachin-Jigar and sung by Atif Aslam. The lyrics of the song urge the listener to let go of past hurt, pain, and regrets and to focus on living in the present and looking to the future. The song also promotes the idea of hope and perseverance, encouraging the listener to keep pushing forward no matter how difficult the journey may be. The slow and emotive melody, coupled with the powerful vocals, help to convey the message of hope and perseverance in moving on from past.

XVI
Maa from Taare Zameen Par

"Maa" from Taare Zameen Par is a song that speaks to the unconditional love and support of a mother, composed by Shankar-Ehsaan-Loy and sung by Shankar Mahadevan. The lyrics of the song pay tribute to the sacrifices and love that a mother gives, and express gratitude towards them. The song promotes the idea of love, support and family, encouraging all to be grateful for the love and support of their mother. The emotive melody and powerful vocals help to convey the message of love and gratitude towards a mother, and the role that they play in shaping and supporting a child's life.

XVII

Kar Har Maidaan Fateh from Sanju

"Kar Har Maidaan Fateh" from Sanju is a song that promotes the idea of perseverance and determination, composed by Vikram Montrose and sung by Sukhwinder Singh. The lyrics of the song urge the listener to never give up, to always push forward, and to strive for success no matter the odds. The song also promotes the idea of facing one's fears and struggles head-on, encouraging the listener to confront and overcome them. The fast-paced beat and powerful vocals of the song help to convey the message of determination and perseverance, which are key in achieving the goal.

XVIII

Maa Tujhe Salaam

"Maa Tujhe Salaam" from Vande Mataram is a patriotic song that speaks to the sacrifices and struggles of the brave people who fought to protect their country, composed by A. R. Rahman and sung by A. R. Rahman. The lyrics of the song pay tribute to the sacrifices made by the soldiers and their families, and express gratitude towards them. The song also promotes the idea of unity and togetherness in the face of adversity, encouraging all citizens to stand together in defense of their country. The emotive melody, powerful vocals, and patriotic lyrics of the song help to convey the message of love for the country and respect for the sacrifices made for it.

XIX

Zinda from Zinda

"Zinda" from Zinda is a song that showcases the motivational aspect of never giving up and always pushing yourself to be the best version of yourself, no matter the circumstances, composed by Anu Malik and sung by Sunidhi Chauhan. The lyrics of the song urge the listener to never give up on their dreams and to always strive to be the best version of themselves, even in the face of adversity. The song also promotes the idea of determination and perseverance, as it encourages the listener to keep pushing forward no matter how difficult the journey may be. The fast-paced beat and powerful vocals of the song help to convey the message of never giving up and always pushing oneself to be the best.

XX

Mitwa from Kabhi Alvida Naa Kehna

"Mitwa" from Kabhi Alvida Naa Kehna is a song that promotes the idea of living in the present and enjoying the beauty of life, composed by Shankar-Ehsaan-Loy and sung by Shankar Mahadevan, KK and Lata Mangeshkar. The lyrics of the song urge the listener to live in the present and to not hold on to the past. The song also encourages the listener to enjoy the beauty of life, and to not be bogged down by regrets or missed opportunities. The upbeat tempo and catchy melody of the song help to convey the message of enjoying life and embracing every moment.

XXI

Maa from Mission Mangal

"Maa" from Mission Mangal is a song that speaks to the sacrifices and struggles of the mother and mother figures, and how they are the backbone of families and society. Composed by Amit Trivedi and sung by Keerthi Sagathia, it pays tribute to the sacrifices and love that mothers give, and express gratitude towards them. The song promotes the idea of love, support and family, encouraging all to be grateful for the love and support of their mother. The emotive melody and powerful vocals help to convey the message of love and gratitude towards a mother and their role in shaping and supporting a child's life.

XXII

Maa from Neerja

"Maa" from Neerja is a song that speaks to the sacrifices and struggles of the mother and mother figures, composed by Vishal Khurana and sung by Sunidhi Chauhan. The lyrics of the song pay tribute to the sacrifices made by the mothers, and express gratitude towards them. The song promotes the idea of love, support and family, encouraging all to be grateful for the love and support of their mother. The emotive melody and powerful vocals help to convey the message of love and gratitude towards a mother and their role in shaping and supporting a child's life.

XXIII

Maa from PK

"Maa" from PK is a song that speaks to the sacrifices and struggles of the mother and mother figures, composed by Shantanu Moitra and sung by Swanand Kirkire. The lyrics of the song pay tribute to the sacrifices made by the mothers, and express gratitude towards them. The song promotes the idea of love, support and family, encouraging all to be grateful for the love and support of their mother. The emotive melody and powerful vocals help to convey the message of love and gratitude towards a mother and their role in shaping and supporting a child's life.

XXIV

Maa from The Sky is Pink

"Maa" from The Sky is Pink is a song that speaks to the sacrifices and struggles of the mother and mother figures, composed by Pritam and sung by Arijit Singh. The lyrics of the song pay tribute to the sacrifices made by the mothers, and express gratitude towards them. The song promotes the idea of love, support and family, encouraging all to be grateful for the love and support of their mother. The emotive melody and powerful vocals help to convey the message of love and gratitude towards a mother and their role in shaping and supporting a child's life.

XXV

Maa from Uri

"Maa" from Uri: The Surgical Strike is a song that speaks to the sacrifices and struggles of the soldiers and their mothers, composed by Shashwat Sachdev and sung by Kumaar. The lyrics of the song pay tribute to the sacrifices made by the soldiers and their mothers, and express gratitude towards them. The song promotes the idea of love, support and sacrifice, encouraging all to be grateful for the sacrifices made by soldiers and their mothers. The emotive melody and powerful vocals help to convey the message of love, gratitude and sacrifice towards the soldiers and their mothers.

XXVI

"Maa" from Lage Raho Munna Bhai

"Maa" from Lage Raho Munna Bhai is a song that speaks to the sacrifices and struggles of the mother and mother figures, composed by Shantanu Moitra and sung by Sonu Nigam. The lyrics of the song pay tribute to the sacrifices made by the mothers, and express gratitude towards them. The song promotes the idea of love, support and family, encouraging all to be grateful for the love and support of their mother. The emotive melody and powerful vocals help to convey the message of love and gratitude towards a mother and their role in shaping and supporting a child's life.

XXVII

"Maa" from Dangal

"Maa" from Dangal is a song that speaks to the sacrifices and struggles of the mother and mother figures, composed by Pritam and sung by Sarwar Khan, Sartaz Khan Barna. The lyrics of the song pay tribute to the sacrifices made by the mothers, and express gratitude towards them. The song promotes the idea of love, support and family, encouraging all to be grateful for the love and support of their mother. The emotive melody and powerful vocals help to convey the message of love and gratitude towards a mother and their role in shaping and supporting a child's life.

XXVIII
Maa from Kabir Singh

"Maa" from Kabir Singh is a song that speaks to the sacrifices and struggles of the mother and mother figures, composed by Sachet-Parampara and sung by Sachet Tandon. The lyrics of the song pay tribute to the sacrifices made by the mothers, and express gratitude towards them. The song promotes the idea of love, support and family, encouraging all to be grateful for the love and support of their mother. The emotive melody and powerful vocals help to convey the message of love and gratitude towards a mother and their role in shaping and supporting a child's life.

XXIX

"Maa" from Bajrangi Bhaijaan

"Maa" from Bajrangi Bhaijaan is a song that talks about the unbreakable bond between a mother and her child. The song is sung by Javed Ali and composed by Pritam. The lyrics, written by Kausar Munir, tell the story of a young boy, Bajrangi, who is lost in Pakistan and his mother's longing for him to return home safely. The song is filled with emotions of longing, love and the hope that Bajrangi's mother has that one day she will be reunited with her son. The song motivates the listener to never give up hope, and to always have faith that things will eventually work out for the best.

ॐ

XXX

"Maa" from Secret Superstar

"Maa" from Secret Superstar is a song about the sacrifices that a mother makes for her child. The song is sung by Meghna Mishra and composed by Amit Trivedi. The lyrics, written by Kausar Munir, tell the story of a young girl, Insiya, who wants to pursue her dream of becoming a singer despite the opposition from her father. The song is a celebration of a mother's love and support, and the unwavering belief that she has in her child. The song inspires the listener to follow their dreams, no matter how difficult the journey may be, and to always have the support of their mother.

XXXI

"Maa" from Hichki

"Maa" from Hichki is a song that is about the mother as a role model. The song is sung by Neuman Pinto and composed by Jasleen Royal. The lyrics, written by Aditya Sharma, tell the story of a teacher, Naina, who is struggling with Tourette Syndrome and her relationship with her mother. The song is a tribute to mothers and the sacrifices they make for their children. It shows how the mother's love and support can give strength to a person even in the toughest of times. The song motivates to believe in oneself, even if the world deems us as weak and to never give up on the dream.

XXXII

"Maa" from Pink

"Maa" from Pink is a song about the power of mother's love. The song is sung by Vidhi Sharma and composed by Shantanu Moitra. The lyrics, written by Tanveer Ghazi, tell the story of three girls who are struggling with the aftermath of a traumatic incident. The song is a tribute to mothers and the sacrifices they make for their children. It shows how a mother's love can help a person heal and move on from difficult situations. The song motivates one to stand up against adversity and injustice and to always have the strength and support of a mother's love to fall back on.

XXXIII

"Maa" from Badhaai Ho

"Maa" from Badhaai Ho is a song that is about the celebration of motherhood and the bond between a mother and her child. The song is sung by Papon and composed by Tanishk Bagchi. The lyrics, written by Vayu, tell the story of a middle-aged couple who are expecting a child, and the song is an ode to mothers and the sacrifices they make for their children. It celebrates the joy and love that a mother brings into a child's life, and the unbreakable bond that exists between them. The song is a reminder that mother's love knows no bounds and it is infinite. The song motivates to cherish the bond with mother and to appreciate her role in life.

XXXIV

"Maa" from Queen

"Maa" from Queen is a song that is about the mother as a role model and the influence she has on her child. The song is sung by Amit Trivedi and composed by Amit Trivedi. The lyrics, written by Anvita Dutt, tell the story of a young girl, Rani, who is struggling to find her identity after her fiancé breaks up with her on the eve of their wedding. The song is a tribute to mothers and the sacrifices they make for their children. It shows how a mother's love and guidance can help a person find the strength and courage to overcome difficult situations and to be independent. The song motivates one to look up to mother as role model to be strong and capable in life.

XXXV

"Maa" from Mary Kom

"Maa" from Mary Kom is a song that is about the mother as a source of inspiration and support. The song is sung by Vishal Dadlani and composed by Shashi Suman. The lyrics, written by Prashant Ingole, tell the story of a young girl, Mary Kom, who is struggling to become a boxer and her relationship with her mother. The song is a tribute to mothers and the sacrifices they make for their children. It shows how a mother's love and support can give a person the strength and determination to chase their dreams and to overcome obstacles. The song is a motivational anthem that encourages listeners to be inspired by the strength and determination of a mother, to chase their dreams and to never give up.

XXXVI

Apna Time Aayega

Gully Boy: The movie has a number of motivational songs such as "Apna Time Aayega", "Jingostan", "Asli Hip Hop" and "Mere Gully Mein" which talks about the struggles of an aspiring rapper and the need to never give up on one's dreams, to believe in oneself, no matter the odds and to rise above the circumstances. These songs were composed by Divine and Ankur Tewari and sung by Ranveer Singh and Divine.

XXXVII

Pepsi Ki Kasam from The Zoya Factor

The Zoya Factor: The movie has a song "Pepsi Ki Kasam" which is a motivational and energetic song which is about to chase your dreams, no matter how impossible they may seem, and to never give up. The song is sung by Shankar Mahadevan and composed by Shankar-Ehsaan-Loy.

Contact

DR. JAGADEESH PILLAI

PhD in Vedic Science

Four Times Guinness World Record Holder

Winner of Mahatma Gandhi Vishwa Shanti Puraskar and
Global Peace Ambassador

Gemology, Astro & Vastu Consultant - Spiritual Counselor

Consultant for designing World Record Ideas

Efficient Tarot Card Reader

9839093003

myrichindia@gmail.com

drjagadeeshpillai@facebook

drjagadeeshpillai@instagram

jagadeeshpillai@youtube

www. JAGADEESHPILLAI.com

|| LOKAHA SAMASTHAHA SUKHINO BHAVANTU ||

• 53 •